America
the
Beautiful

Selected Works by Paula Gunn Allen

Novels:

The Woman Who Owned The Shadows

Poetry:

Blind Lion

A Cannon Between My Knees

Shadow Country

Skin and Bones

Life is a Fatal Disease: Collected Poems

Critical Studies and Memoir:

*The Sacred Hoop:Recovering the Feminine
in American Indian Tradition*

Spider Woman's Granddaughter

As Long As the Rivers Flow: The Stories of Nine Native Americans

Pocahontas: Medicine Woman, Spy, Entrepreneur, Diplomat

Grandmothers of the Light: A Medicine Woman's Sourcebook

*Off the Reservation: Reflections on Boundary-Busting,
Border-Crossing Loose Cannons*

America
the
Beautiful

Last Poems

Paula Gunn Allen

West End Press

2010

First edition, July 2010
Paperback ISBN 978-0-9816693-5-9

Book Design by Bryce Milligan
Cover art by Karen Thomason Darr.
Author photograph by Melinda Fay

For book information, see our Web site at
www.westendpress.org

West End Press
P.O. Box 27334
Albuquerque, NM 87125

Contents

To the Reader, by Patricia Clark Smith   *vii*

America the Beautiful

Apache Warrior – Apache Troop	2
America the Beautiful I	6
America the Beautiful II	8
America the Beautiful III	9
America the Beautiful IV	10
America the Beautiful V	12
America the Beautiful VI	14
America the Beautiful VII	15
America the Beautiful VIII	17
America the Beautiful IX	19
America the Beautiful X	20
America the Beautiful XI	22
America the Beautiful XII	24
America the Beautiful XIII	25
America the Beautiful XIV	26
America the Beautiful XV	29
America the Beautiful XVI	34
America the Beautiful XVII	35
America the Beautiful XVIII	36
America the Beautiful XIX	38
America the Beautiful XX	40
America the Beautiful XXI	42
America the Beautiful XXII	43
America the Beautiful XXIII	44
America the Beautiful XXIV	45
America the Beautiful XXV	46
America the Beautiful XXVI	48
America the Beautiful XXVII	50
America the Beautiful XXVIII	51
America the Beautiful XXIX	52
America the Beautiful XXX	53

America the Beautiful XXXI   54
America the Beautiful XXXII   55
America the Beautiful XXXIII   56
America the Beautiful XXXIV   57
America the Beautiful XXXV   59
America the Beautiful XXXVI   60
America the Beautiful XXXVII   61
America the Beautiful XXXVIII   62

There is Another Shore

The Kingdom of Nye   66
Three   68
Another Shore   69
Sin Verguenza   71
Wayward Girl's Lament   74
Skyscape   75
Values   76
Still Crazy   78
Self Portrait and a Wish   80
Dawn Sneaks   81
I Understand When I Watch TV   83
coyote rhymester on the lam   84
All the Same Beans   86
Which Way's Up, Doc?   88
Borrachitarme Voy   90
SE FUE (He Left [Himself])   91
Minding the Gap   92
Treasured   94
Love Poem   95
How Near, How Far   97

A Note on the Text, by John Crawford   99

To the Reader

I am sitting beside our small backyard fishpond in Albuquerque's North Valley, remembering Paula, who passed over on May 29, 2008.

When she was back here in New Mexico, she usually stayed with me and John, and she liked it out here at the pond. For one thing, she could smoke, which she could not inside our house. That wasn't all, of course. She was always taken by ecosystems, and here was a small-scale one right at her feet, one she could enjoy observing while sitting down and smoking. She cackled, hearing the Woodhouse's toads rasping their raucous love songs, and feeding the gape-mouthed goldfish. She loved cattails, and dragonflies, and the sound of running water, Laguna Pueblo-Lebanese desert girl that she was.

Today there is a new generation of tadpoles swarming around the verge of the pond gobbling algae, waiting to morph. Paula embraced the idea and the fact of transformation. Again, the yellow water flags are coming up on their little island. And the tamarisk, that invader-tree from the Middle East now declared illegal in New Mexico, is starting to leaf out in its feathery fearless immigrant way.

Paula loved irises—her Laguna grandma grew them, over in Cubero, NM. Paula had a special liking for the one named Supreme Sultan by its growers, who comes out, out OUT, in outrageous gold and crimson splendor. She was so delighted to learn that Supreme Sultan in my haphazard iris bed is flanked by ruffly pink Miss Beverly Sills, and tough little Brown Lasso. She always said my irises sounded like the cast of a bad 1940's musical, or a parade in the Castro.

Many of my memories of Paula involve her great big pomposity-destroying laughter. As Joy Harjo once said to me, it was a laugh you could hear two classrooms away, even with the doors closed.

Paula and I first met in the mailroom of the English Department at the University of New Mexico in Albuquerque, thanks to her professor, David Remley, who was instrumental in first getting her published. She was massively pregnant in a purple-flowered maternity dress, and I had a toddler hanging on to my thumb. We took one look at one another and just started laughing before we said a word. We knew we were not what aspiring graduate students and untenured professors were supposed to look like. But it was more; a real laughter of recognition, one many people experienced with Paula. Oh, Hi! Gee, guess we will be friends forever!

We went on to do a lot of work together, some side-by-side, some co-written. In time, my husband John Crawford would become the main publisher of her poetry. She really wanted this book to be in his hands.

Three things about Paula:

First, her myriadmindedness, as James Joyce would have said. Of course she was interested in all one would expect her to care about--feminist issues, Native history and storytelling, family stories from both Lebanon and Laguna, gay struggles. But she was also so passionate about cutting-edge physics, strange etymology, pop culture—you name it. Her favorite song was always "Don't Fence Me in." I wish you might have heard her about string theory, or the Gene Autry Museum, both of which she loved.

Secondly, her sheer playfulness. Our house is filled with toys she sent us over the years: an extremely soft teddy bear, a pre-Barbie girl doll from the 40's, a ceramic rabbit with tiny baby rabbits inside that always sits on our Easter table. We are talking about a woman who could never resist a yard sale, never stop buying friends presents, and God knows could never keep away from a bad pun.

And then there is her courage. This manuscript was completed and sent to West End as Paula was awaiting the death she knew was coming from lung cancer. She faced many other tough things in her life. Coming out, for one: liberating, of course, but also difficult. It got easier—in later years, she would describe herself as "a serial bisexual." She endured the SIDS of an infant, and the equally unexpected death of her adult son Gene, her own illness, a devastating house fire. Her surviving children, Lauralee and Suliman, and the many communities of people whom she touched sustained her.

We hope this last book will recall her wonderful heart, mind, and spirit to you. Since Paula did not leave us with a dedication, though she was always scrupulous about giving thanks, it is for you, reader.

Patricia Clark Smith
Albuquerque, NM
April, 2010

Publisher's Note: Patricia Clark Smith died on July 11, 2010. See remarks in "A Note on the Text," at the end of this volume. The dedication Pat suggests in the last paragraph above will have to stand as coming from her and myself, her husband.

WORKSHOP: ESSAY #4

The Prompt Essay #4: An introduction to a 20thC American Woman Poet. Suggested length: 6-8 typed pages, including works cited page. Workshop: complete typed draft due in class May 15. Final essay: due during scheduled final exam time: 2-4:00 pm, Friday May 17. In this essay you will introduce a 20th century American woman poet, providing a brief biography, an overview of her work in poetry, and a close reading of a representative poem. Your overview might include a discussion of any of the following in her work: common themes, formal choices, important cultural contexts, publication issues, critical debates, influences--etc! You should preface your analysis of a representative poem with a brief explanation of your reasons for choosing this poem in particular.

1. Read through your partner's essay, putting checks in the margin next to anything awkward, unclear, wordy, or fabulous. Discuss.

2. Read through the prompt, above. Which parts of the prompt does the essay do well? Where? Which parts might the writer address more fully?

3. Look at the original poem—read it together and ask your partner questions about it. Where in the essay is analysis of the poem most insightful? Are formal elements discussed? Where might a line, an image, a line break, a metaphor, a sound (etc!) be more fully explored?

4. Look at the opening of each paragraph in the essay: it is clear what will follow? Is the subject of the paragraph connected back to the goals of the essay? Could it be?

5. Can you explain clearly why the paragraphs in the essay are in this order? Can you imagine any other order?

6. Look at citations—do you have any questions about format? Check a citation guide at http://libraryguides.stolaf.edu/english . Be sure the period in each sentence comes AFTER the parenthetical citation.

7. Suggest one goal for your partner's revision work.

SEE YOU FRIDAY AFTERNOON!

America
the
Beautiful

Apache Warrior – Apache Troop

. . . zone reconnaissance
state of the art – tank –
stabilized sight, stabilized gun
15 to whatever miles an hour
bouncing along like this
23 tons of steel wrapped around
a marvel of new engineering
blows you away

Kiowa helicopters
low flying skimming not far in the dust above maybe 50 feet
survey in front of the tanks maybe six miles out
but usually closer
first taste of battle, first blood
the reporter says
the camera sweeps over
lines of armored pumped young men
making their way across the Iraqi desert
Third Infantry, Seventh Cavalry

at higher speeds they fire more accurately
they carry classified numbers of shells
armor piercing some of them
high explosive some of them

are you scared yet?

Crazy Horse Troop
just ahead, Bone Crusher just behind,
flying reconnaissance for oncoming tanks
the Warriors in the Seventh Helicopters
two women fly
one a West Point graduate who survived 20 rapes

thinks it's a real hoot to be the first to see
the enemy,

I can just imagine
Rommel in the desert but you couldn't do it then
there were no WARRIORS in WWII
they couldn't talk to each other real time,
no night sights, no moving shots,
couldn't flee and fight at the same time

things are so different now
you wonder how they got through
but they did,
they were
through, that is
maybe because they couldn't see

none of us really knew the plan
if any of us really knew the plan
if we could just get there quickly
establish a beachhead there

in the oldest desert of western man
the movement across the desert
the oasis of war
as old as the sands
we thought we knew the plan
but they didn't do what we said they'd do

what they said they'd do
Washington said
you aren't following the plan

you don't have a plan,
the commander snapped
and that was true

Tomahawk missile up, up and away, shot
by the photographer bouncing on the hood
of the Warrior as he takes these historic pictures
for the historic Seventh Cavalry
Captain somebody from somewhere Texas
you all come out of there with your hands up like Sheridan said

this commander's precursive self said chasing
other heathens in fields of blood and buffalo grass;
this one 26, 27 maybe, never in battle before –
and those 18, 19 year olds he leads
all wound up, adrenaline high, MRE,
no sleep, only the desert and the threat of gas,
nightmares of World War I, the corpse and rat filled trenches,
although postmodern warriors lie in single holes all suited up.
It's crowded and close in there and who knows how many
more days to go
we're just doing what's right the baby faced warrior claims,
like we've always done since so long ago.

"Garryowen" was Custer's marching song
has always been the Seventh Cavalry's

them who were wiped out by the Sioux
in different times of course, defeated then
like to be defeated now, say "Garryowen",
the Seventh will respond,
HOO HAA

is that from Texas, or Gary, Indiana,
or maybe all the way from Geronimo's grave?

The most important thing when the shit goes down
it's good to have something good to hold on to
a unit with a proud history you can write home about
a motto, a battle cry of your own

I bet when they began to move troops into Iraq
at the cessation of their apocryphal "Shock and Awe,"
some Commander said into his microphone
Heads up, people. We're going into Indian Country.
That was how they began the invasion of Kuwait a decade before.
And in battle after battle preceding through two centuries.
Why not this decade, this century too.

March 2003

America the Beautiful I

compose
discompose
decompose
recompose
expos
expose
indispose
overexpose
predispose
preexpose
propose
reimpose
suppose
superimpose
superpose
transpose
underexpose

when you take a position, even assumptively
you might find your disposition presumptively
supposition suppository; suppose
that's because what you have on deposit
has probably been deposed
say, hey! reposition the composition
hid it in the repository
that's stashed in the depository
so when they posit this new approach,
make propositions and find new topics to broach,
you can bet they have a preposition
way beyond your wildest suppositions
which of course shows them preposterous
which is what they leave to posterity

beyond the reach of obfuscation, iteration,
bodacious boisterous imposture's repository

L: *pausa*: to stop; to rest;
in some of them, from *ponere*, to put: e.g., depose, to put down.
    (pony up, dude)
depose, dispose: L. *prae positer;* before-put and/or down-put,
out-put the dog
place, placement, order, organization + prepositional sites of
    these;

rhymes with **pose**
arapahos; navajos; anglos; buffalos; jingoes; manifestoes;
pueblos; shalakos; ufos; chicas y chicos; todos los pendejos

Fort Bragg 2004

America the Beautiful II

poseur, poser, posture
dispose, oppose
opposite
apposite
apostate
post haste

not expose, impose
no repose, depose

the power, the posture,
the disposition of the imposition
exposition 1932 World Fair
st louie, louie, some other
everywheres pleasured

only a rose, what is repose
what body posture is not opposed
what empire is not exposed
what government is indisposed
can be deposed, reposed
impostered, imposured,
measured, treasured,
not ever to be deposed.

Fort Bragg 2004

America the Beautiful III

are you of the earth, the soft wind asked
no I answered I am of somewhere else
the sky maybe, beyond it maybe
I know, because I dream

are you aware the earth dreams, the summer surf asked
no I answered, the earth is the third rock from the sun
filled with carbon-based life forms to be sure
but still a rock for all that

are you aware that rocks dream, the deep night stars asked
no I answered, they can't dream. I know because
rocks can't move and they can't think.
rocks don't know god

are you aware that god doesn't move, asked the quasar songs
from the edge of the universe
no, I answered,
I am aware of the rocks, they're not aware of me.
I am aware of the earth, it's not aware of me.

how do you know they aren't aware of you?
that they don't move, dance, dream?
if they didn't how could you
do
     any
         thing?

May 18, 2004

America the Beautiful IV

do you remember the time
when buffalo stood lonely
and still cast in nickel
and the trickle of water
from the drying spring
and the blue speckled eggs
the robins left to bake
in a twiggy bake-lite oven
they called a nest
ok, we called it that
they called it home
however birds indicate
whatever it is they cogitate
they as well as bovines meditate
like the lone bison
a collection item now

time is a rhyming thing
which i suppose in the algebra
of wisdom means
space rhymes as well
trochee? spondee?
surely not iamb
i am not either
poetry is what be's
(h'mmm)
regardless of intent
can do nothing because
that's not the point
anymore than the buffalo
time out of rhyme
out of mind
out of my pocket into the gap

of which we must be mindful
cast in nickel if there is still
such a thing and we much think
about trickers, ticklers, sticklers
coyote laps

2005

America the Beautiful V

despond
the slough
we slew the ancients
stole burned lost
disposed and deposed
and all for what
responding is futile
resistance a joke
water flows as it goes
you all know
and correspondence
is thick and unmoved
what matches what
little girl dead of snow
nothing but pure white heart
to show for all of it except
the cooked goose and lighted tree
spondee, another trick
a rhetoric, a flick of the bic
a click no butter can melt
despite or because
the flaming was for those
of sinister dexterity silenced
by decades and centuries
when pilgrims watched the pyres
a sort of way to respond
unkindly, kinder, tinder, kin,
you'd think there was another
way and you'd be wrong
despondence and dependence
John Bull turned
into a gentleman nerd
matches were lucifers now recycled

cardboard that makes no lucky
strikes. better tinder. better winter.
better cross the slough
and get out of dodge

America the Beautiful VI (aside)

I agree that american notions are far from the mark
teachings but how does one sort the wheat from the chaff.
not throw out the baby with the bath water.

I know that a bird in the hand is worth ten in the bush,
a stitch in time saves nine, and fifty-five saves lives.
men of knowledge agree, damn fools,
it's better to have loved and lost than not to have loved at all.

And he who laughs last laughs best, so what I say is
pack up your troubles in your old kit pack and remember
it's hard to soar with the eagles when you're surrounded by dreck.

2004

America the Beautiful VII

it's the petunia of the spirit that remains,
along with noble phlox, tenacious lobelia,
stubborn dandelion, small cedar, scrub oak.
the streets today are hot in this little town
going big time. new crosswalks,
high rents in this worker's paradise
where labor's cheap and gas costs high.
we live on the rocky shores of earth's greatest sea.
where the earth's greatest pines used to grow,
where rhododendrons bloom like giant trees of light
providing opportunity for one and all to take
the easy way out – one bright petal salad
and you're gone. well-bred roses here are grown
in pens to keep out deer (although wild ones bloom free).
here as elsewhere I've learned that when white-out fluid
thickens it mucks up the line, blurs the print:
I know that rivers can get that way too.
surely you remember the nations' vow:
as long as the rivers flow?
(surely you don't)
and more, they vowed: as long as the
grass grows. sometimes I long for
begonias, daffodils, honeysuckle, lilacs
out of time I like the way they
set off neon and honky-tonk
highlight scat and rap. make a statement
with bluegrass and blues.

in the center of our town there's a trophy:
I saw it only by accident though it had been
there for more than a hundred years
maybe less. A huge chunk of redwood trunk,

huge saws mounted against its vastness,
as though to say: look what hungry
family men armed with steel can do.
the dead-tree bisected by the steel that downed it
guards the mansion that's now historical site
where photos of leading townsmen
longago hang...not one hungry family man,
all well-fed, stern, sleek...

beneath the new surface of trendy shops
and friendly folks invisible war is waged:
war on red woods, war on red
people, war on poverty
and impoverished, war on drugs,
war on war. there must be a place
for free range deer
for grass growing wild and free
for lobelia and fuchsias, for deathly
rhododendrons, for longing and rage
in this place of seven thousand
mad whited-out souls and three
hundred mad indians nobody recognizes.
just look around and see what is now, what
should be, could have been, what's the use.
there is reason enough for indians to go mad
whited out over centuries. for water
to get sullen and refuse to flow. for
grass to sulk. even the sky is crazy with rage.
even the earth's gone mad.

Spring 2005

America the Beautiful VIII

gentlewoman, mother earth
bitch goddess and her son
game invidious now afoot
never gentle, never sweet
furious ever stark repose,
angry bird, tearing beak
disheveled but beloved
ever formless ever grief
rusting sandstone mesas
enraging whatever touches them
bleached beyond respect
rock washed surf and shore
never mended
ended insolvent,
abject, no reprieve

who's there to share
whatever they're
giving out today
smells like roses
tastes like shit.

aromatic despair
where water striders
waterweb once offered sweet
cold earth filtered drink
now dead, now dry
now old trading post stands still
sandstone walls and char
turmoil surfs brown and dingy
where the deeps should profoundly stretch
vast into the sky roiling dissettlement

one can wish the tide went both ways
taking whatever's ejected by the sea
clear clean away
ancient highway closing in
no lollipop trees, no
psilocybin seas
no dreams of me
no songs of thee

Fort Bragg 2005

America the Beautiful IX

despite the sun,
tanning bars, protection make-up,
we get whiter all the time
bleed-out the spirit that can't go on
violet rejects chlorine sprays
which make noticeable the death
their very pallor brings
say: it's bad for mother earth

as though crazed that ancient dame
created chemicals dangerous to herself so we
could vilify their use
and there find our own redemption
only the spirit that loses color
that goes pasty-grey beneath
plastic glow is perilous in itself
wants recognition to be absolved

i have seen lots where new growth
trees were held hostage in corrals
where mutant heather ate the hills
where pristine grasses fled the sea
i have seen the sun bleating like a lost lamb
wanting to be found, saved, brought home
i have seen winter unaware of itself
whisper to camellias, poinsettias, maple leaves

i have wondered who makes the rules
draws the harrowing pictures qua facts
for us to contemplate with morning tea
non caffeinated to assuage our fear and rage

Fort Bragg, September 13, 2004

America the Beautiful X

the sand pounds the surf, huge rocks swallow spray
it is not their first breath and surely not the last.
sister stones raise their noses to the air
the rest of their vastness hidden modestly beneath the waves
a sunstung day

on the eve of yesterday the flowers lowered their faces
and grimaced at the sanitized ground of their being
sadness radiating because they were fastened to one place.
but when fog or rain fell they knew
they would face the sun
serene because their children
would wander far before
getting trapped in their turn

look.
there's a furry bit of blood smearing the asphalt.
rabbit? chipmunk? squirrel?
look.
those pines are laden with disease.
shameful
they don't cover the powdery crud
clinging to their boughs
shameful
they don't bow their heads
stand ersatz proud
as if they were nobility

always wishing for a better place unsettled minds cast lots
like the god genius pushed away while clacking dice
chattering up the night made a gamer's day.
I want to ask the trees
if they're wishing they could move.

do they want to talk faster
go farther
get more.
I wonder where trees stash their stuff,
why they let vermin covered critters use them
casually
and cast them off

whether any bird, squirrel, chipmunk, lichen, insect,
any or all remember to say thanks –
did they have good mothers
to teach them to be polite
or were they raised
in a barn?

on the beach and inland as high as the high high hills
the rocks to about their enduring business shutting out
the noise of transients –
butterflies
ants
termites
me.
I wish I could ask
how it is to live in more dimensions than one
if simultaneity is the same as timelessness
if I could think or speak s o s l o w l y
whatever they might say
I wouldn't hear.

June 16-21 2004

America the Beautiful XI

perfect
prefect
defect
infect
de fecto? de *fac*to oh.
so no fectless
but feckless
reckless
restless
nestle
mess
fess up
it's useless
factoring in all the elements
who can say which reality is so
real in quantities that
quanta quantify
by which one might identify
and ever and ever rest

it isn't as though we didn't know the crunch
was coming, was here. some speak of ending
times, others of new ages. some announced
new worlds of order as though evoking
or invoking massive earth changes
tsunamis that knock the earth silly
change our orbit, obit, some mess
this bit. i heard that this happened last century
the Great San Francisco Earthquake
wasn't only a movie making Jeannette McDonald
and Clark Gable immortal, no. perfect as
they were, and the special effects so overpowering

I never forgot it. couldn't sleep in the City by the Bay
ran home to rock solid Albuquerque, where wouldn't you know
we had our own rare quake
making my soul to my toes shake.
seeing a solid brick floor in a sunken stone
and adobe house wave at you is unsettling for sure;
in that stunning moment the century revolved
as though even earth kept time by the Gregorian calendar
so as the City quivered over the next few months
things went boom all over.
"the butterfly effect occurs in geology" the writer says.
so hey, everybody: nobody breathe, okay?

Fort Bragg 2005

America the Beautiful XII

Veneration
Venial
Venery
Venus
Venable
ivy and grasses twining about
marble half destroyed chips lying
strewn about a bit of nose, a tendril
of hair, piece of finger, thumb, gown,
coiffure, thick curls wrapped in twine
only Grecian, graceful, venerable

little enough in this new land to rate
any veneration, not even veniality
too grand a condition for petty greed
status war puffed up chests cooing
of me   no clean stone to fall chipped to earth
not even that righteous return
venereal, rose thou art sick,
lovers don't trick lovers into gonorrhea, crabs,
syphilis, HIV-AIDS, however dappled the grove
however ancient the eyes

America the Beautiful XIII

extrude
the magnitude
whether in fugue
or what they call clarity
in which nonsense
passes for lovely décor
Malibu Mendocino Boulder
Santa Fe no shape surrounded
design faction fractional
such
exactitude

here and now *le deluge*
after which who knows
birds will sing no doubt
and the flowers, will do
whatever it's time to do
whether from gratitude
or the simplest of impulses
sine, cosine, otherwise known
as creation of a universe
that curves forever in such ways
we call infinitude
as if

June 8, 2005

America the Beautiful XIV

who will defend the defenseless
against the indefensible?
once it was the queen,
gods save her, but they didn't,
so she can't

because
be
      CAWS
            CAWS
                  CAWS
  cause

one thing causes another
or would if there was only one thing
or another
but linear laterality
must give way to the facts of the matter
as they stand today

fuzzy

FUZZ
      FUZZ
            FUZZ

ravens roost high in the trees
where the wealthy and shaven
brows over their peas
broccoli, arugula, basil and sage
and imagine they're surely among the saved

they haven't heard the queen is a snake
or a dragon, all scaly, for goodness sake
they must have forgotten that it was St. George
who by god's benevolence forced her to change
and forever suffer the unhealed wound.
so men took over, saying she was unclean –
not knowing how again and again,
miraculous woman, could bleed seven days
out of twenty-eight whenever the moon went
secret and dark. no goddess she, demonic plague,
must be a snake, evil inchoate,
heavens, how ill

the ravens are ravening high in the hills
they hide their agendas in the thickness of pines
no one could guess what those big birds have planned
unless you're an Indian from the ends of the land
or a queen bleeding endlessly over the lot,
or sipping her tea, or playing a diverting game of charade
with her queenly companions name Tom, Dick and Bob.

I heard the birds chatting when I drove by today
I pretended I hadn't known what they said
I just kept driving, keeping my head
or my thoughts to myself in that incoherent way
I've cultivated diligently
Every damned day
since I was a child out on a limb
and learned a hard lesson, to my great chagrin,
that almost anyone's smarter than me –
that birds are the smartest and they're the most free
because
they have a cause

a
                CAWS
                            CAWS
                                    CAWS

that's
neither linear, lateral, not earthbound at all.
maybe the ravens will do the great deed
defend the defense and god bless the queen

                                        February 2006

America the Beautiful XV

here it is – our last chance:
saloon hotel gas pump

                              before the grueling
                                    mohave

desert dwellers including
Saddam are not
                      disarming
any oasis can be
                startled
                        a
                      wake
                              ning dream

game OVEROVEROVER
(tomorrow
(another week or two
(a month   max

            remind
            s me of the fifties
            family and drive west every year
            (or as many as daddy could
                              take

[FLAGSTAFF ARIZONA]

three a.m. Headed down to the desert
to arrive before dawn. it wasn't the end of
anything then, Y'all come out of there
with yer hands up

'cause nits breed lice notwithstanding

– we pretend never happened –

(no cold war along that lonesome hiway
(no atomic bombs no
        air-conditioned cats
        no four-lane freeway
        mother make her stop
        move over you fat pig
            california here I come sewanee
            blackbird bye bye

our squabbles fill the empty miles
driven through the killing heat
hollering *if you ever plan to motor west*

      DON'T

[KINGMAN]

SQUEALING WITH HILARITY AT OUR WIT
faces crazy   red and swollen

     YOU KIDS! QUIET DOWN BACK THERE!

Heading into the blazing
          high noon sun
              do not forsake me oh my darling
           (mohave. joshua trees. lizard in the grass.
          there's no grass dummy
Inyo, Twenty-Nine Palms, Salome-Where-She-Danced

(nobody mentioned her taunting the saint
            "the Dance of the Seven Veils" (parents grin in
the   front seat

I can almost hear Uncle Joe   playing the derbukke*
            Uncle Lias   chanting high Arabic
in the crowded car   the rising heat
            all day I face the barren waste
the bloody head of the saint--
            I found out later   high school now

I wonder:
      maybe
the fanatic saint looked like Saddam or
like my dad   who   if he had a thick mustache
would
      (look
            like Saddam
who might
      (look like Mar Hanna** come again
if Saddam or my dad never shaved-- -- who knows?
            I'm the Sheik   of Araby
played at the Casa Marina every time biye, daddy, entered

      (talk about the last chance hotel--
                  bartender, desk clerk, whore and all
                  closed down tight for day
                  opened only nights
                  nobody mentions the ladies of the night

[BARSTOW]

climbing   climbing
                out of the dry dry sea
engine heating almost over
heating
swoop down Sierra rising from sea beds on each side
towering high   as waves   at the beach tower

[SAN BERNARDINO]

glide
        glazed
                    into smog rich air
i still believe is the happy-ever-after-smell of

[CALIFORNIA]

        all asleep on the broad back seat
        tired of going
        tired of singing
        tired of squabbling
        tired of laughing

how deep is the ocean
we're on our way to somewhere
I'd like to leave it all behind and go find

BURMA SHAVE

i can't give you anything   but love   ba-by

past anticipating
ready to wait
ready to get out and play

     cool, clear water

                        let us pray

BOP BOP

* derbukke – Lebanese musical instrument

** Saint John (The Baptist)

America the Beautiful XVI

Rendering to Caesar what is Caesar's and to god what is god's
I watch cnn moneyline and listen to some opera on cd player
      via my pc.
Rendering to Caesar even the language I choose, the part of god
is the moment I am struck and pause. Silence. Chest fills
Eyes grow tears. Still.

I found the cd in a pile of stuff. Its title, *The Greatest Show on
      Earth.*
For months it sat on my desk waiting for the time I would check
      it out.
Today I was needing desk space. It's Christmas, nearly so. The
      news is
obnoxious. And the sounds of Caesar everywhere
bring me neither peace nor cheer. Even the deer don't know what
      time it is
it seems; not one wears antlers. Not one has a glowing red nose.

I don't know who is singing. There is a line in a song the title of
      which I do
not know, although I recognize the melody, the soprano rendering
      her aria.
Tosca? Carmen? The last word, co-*si,*
Sticks in my brain and in my sinews, old and drooping as they
      may be,
growing tangles as my hair grows thin. There are moments
driving near the ocean watching the surf pound its way inland
or listening in on the soft gossip of the great trees that I will
      remember,
The pause, then,
Co-*si.*

Fort Bragg, December 2006

America the Beautiful XVII

it thrives on being in the right
the fire that fuels the tyrant's might
and poets fall into cliché
in imitation of the news today
the shouting bullies brandish writ
to prove that loving's only fit
for male to do to female what he likes
her sacred duty bow to right
the bushes burn almighty bright
illiterate mobs fired up in light
of stupid texts long dead and gone
but freedom's flame that burned so long
is near extinguished in the light
of brighter fires burned for the right
a tedious story told long ago
and told again it's always so
whenever humans come in sight
of real progression -- comes the light
of burning flesh and fear untold
of flaring faggots, bright and bold
I wish it didn't sound so trite
to holler "fire!" to folks packed tight
together in a screaming brawl
that grows consuming fireball
I find within me growing fright
the mobs colluding to excite
death on the streets in holy cause
they swear by god to kill us all
if we continue to insist
in name of love, we must resist
their rage, our fear.

January 19, 2004

America the Beautiful XVIII

have you noticed how much fish
and dreams have in common –
schooled but staying the course,
nibbling here, nibbling there,
male fish doing the reproductive chores,
babysitting and all? have you seen
how big ones hide beneath deep shadowed banks,
round river stones
and wait for fat fly or fisher to fool?
have you watched them flickering in and out
of drifting fronds of green?

have you been out
on a warm day or cold
walking or biking
near a river or a pond
and felt the air on your skin
making you sweat or shiver
and wish you could dive in,
cool off or get warm,
find some hale fellows well met
to share the time?

fish do amazing things under ice, near
volcanoes, in places no man has dared –
they breathe water and never fear
dehydration.

have you noticed fish
floating on the surface of the water
moving as the water moves
inexorably downstream,

or laps serene on smooth or rocky shore,
flopping convulsive on the grass
and then unconscious –
seen in that dying fish
a somber reflection of your dreams?

January 19, 2004

America the Beautiful XIX

Such times appear and reappear like the dogs
who chased the deer through the yard just beyond my fence
raw wood, falling over, very dashing that fence. When
the deer disappeared beyond the tall tangled leafy wall
that untrimmed trees and bushes connived
to shape, they exited stage left. The dogs that entered stage
right
lost the track. Seeking, they crossed the footlights
slipped the fence and bounded to my door
for a chat

Small dog came inside and tried to jump on my bed,
so delighted with his find he tried to turn himself inside out,
while big dog, certain of his mission,
disappeared and reappeared,
reminding his companion of the hunt
circling my singularly undashing yard
that ever remains the same.

Complexities and connivance can
pretzel endlessly leading from nothing
to nowhere,
I have made my precarious peace with them –
connivance, complexity and dash. That is,
I find I am sometimes bereft of the one or the other.
Sometimes of them all

The deer was dashing as another –
which was perhaps the first –
leapt through the small wilderness
three fourths enclosed by tall heavy-leafed branches
just beyond my sliding glass door
no dogs in sight.

Complexities are from another time, say,
our teens, our twenties, the Renaissance,
the Great Plague, WWII or even WWIII;
Certainties are just as rare
twisted, as they are, salted, baked, forever undashed.

May 17/22 2004

America the Beautiful XX

sand pounds the surf as the huge beach rocks breath.
it is not their first breath and surely not the last.
in the near distance sister stones raise their noses to the air
the rest of their vastness hidden modestly beneath the waves
it is a sunstruck day

on the eve of yesterday the flowers lowered their faces
and made moues at the sanitized ground of their being.
they were sad, realizing they were fastened to one place.
but only for now. when fog or rain fall their way they face
the sun, serenely knowing their children wander far
before getting settled in their turn

look. there's a furry bit of blood smearing the asphalt.
Rabbit? Coyote? Squirrel?
look. those pines are laden with disease, shameful that they
don't try to hide the clinging lightness caking their boughs,
shameful that they don't have the wit to bow their heads
that they stand ersatz proud as if they were kings
always wishing for a better place unsettled minds casts lots
like the God Einstein pushed away, refusing the clacking of dice
could chatter up the night and make a gaming day.

I want to ask the trees if they wish they could move.
do they want to talk faster, go
farther, get more?
I wonder where trees stash their stuff, and why
they let vermin covered critters use them casually
and cast them off

does any bird, squirrel, chipmunk, lichen, insect, any or all
remember to say thanks? do they walk in reverence, balanced,

singing the imagined song of harmony? did they have good
mothers who taught them manners? are they spiritual
as only organic natural can be?
or were they raised in a barn, grown into unrepentant degenerates?

on the beach and inland as high as the high high hills
the rocks go about their rocky business
shutting out the noise of transient butterflies,
ants, chickadees and me. I would like to ask
how it feels to live in more than one place at a time
but I can't hear or speak so slow.
whatever they might say I would never hear.

June 10, 2004

America the Beautiful XXI

For Ethel

The ineffable mother, daughter, ghost
corn grown tall,
ripened,
withered,
fallen,
passed on clan mother role to me
oak continuing as oaks do

receiving rain with silent grace
"come here and look," she beckons
she's standing at the deep kitchen window
outer frame sky blue to ward evil spirits
and I stand beside her
gaze at the tall beautiful mountain
the Woman Who Comes from the North
Tse'pina, shaven peak reaching toward the Thunderheads
powerful, delicate as a sparrow, hawk, never small
eagle huge as setting sun casts sidelong light
mountain circling high above

everything's breathing, even us.

July/Oct 2006

America the Beautiful XXII

empty the streets frozen stiff
deep night when hope is a dead letter drop
I huddle awake and dreaming
watching the frosted haze swirl
around the dim streetlight down the block
knowing that when I might see
can't matter any more
than I.

June 15, 2002

America the Beautiful XXIII

I guess I walked right into it,
the door. I could have sworn it was open.
I was sure I had been invited over for a meal. I saw
smiles, smelled welcome odors of a fine repast –
milk and honey for a hungry heart.
I guess I walked right into that.

There was me, sailing up the walk,
beaming, bearing wine and flowers,
so happy to be asked. If I'd had a tail
it would have been wagging. If I'd had the apparatus
I would have purred.

How on earth could I have imagined all that –
open door, welcoming face,
inviting aromas flavoring the air,
suffusing it with cilantro and garlic, chocolate, butter and
cream –
the seeming door that opened wide
was made of glass.
The light I thought was welcoming me
a mere reflection of setting sun:
that glare.

Fort Bragg 2004

America the Beautiful XXIV

meditation while watching MSNBC

something mistaken, something unexplained,
something forgotten, a barely echoing refrain,
something left over from another place –
was it mercy? was it grace?
whatever it was, it was very small,
barely in the picture at all
nothing too obvious, a moth or a fly,
a new blade of grass, a quickly hushed cry,
I hardly noticed although it was me,
a memory hidden since I was three –
something flashing by on mind's screen –
wild geese flying, lone eagle on the wing,
small branch flung off in a hurricane gale,
green twig sent twisting in a tornado trail
someone or something I can't remember which
mother? daddy? light suddenly flicks
off on, off on. or maybe that's just how it seems.
maybe none of it happened outside of bad dreams
no one remembers, so who's to say
how heavy the light, how brilliant the gray?

August 2, 2005

America the Beautiful XXV

Cocktail Hour

barring sinister dexterity
the poet's quip
all will go as thought:
we will belly up and hoist a few
waiting
celebrating.

(is it precious? was it good?)

our night leaks intermittent light
garish
revealing
what is otherwise obscured

nothing sinister in the
discoloring glare
indeed, rather
a pulsing neon lullaby
soothing

graceful to the eye
whatever
at the bar
we hold dear:
sweet juicy maraschino
tart spurting lime
inexorably leaves

closing time
arrives so
bleary and dizzy
hardly able to move
left   or   right

leaving us staggered
half blind

January 20, 2004

America the Beautiful XXVI

For Harry Hay
d. October 24, 2002

A week no more or less
I spend talking on the ether
about my fairy fay

fey the discussion
fey the undaunted insistence
time, place, proof, incidence

all that to hear
the fairy godmother died
that exact day

and all the hours and verbiage
all the years and courage
what passes for study

Faugh! pretension
Fie! on disbelief
clap, clap, and spit in the wind

(something passes beneath the high hill
something moves faster than breath
on the stored air)

I thought there were heroes,
that I knew their echoes
sounding from canyon walls

I thought something beckoned
vacant halls, spirit arches,
crystal whirring wings

October 27, 2002

America the Beautiful XXVII

What's a lert? I asked.
I dunno, was the reply,
except it takes on different shades.
The lert today is orange,
and, they say, it's huge.

A huge orange lert.

Does it have long pointy ears?
Is it furred, does it have elephant-type hide?
Maybe it has teeth that get sharper
as its colors change.
Is it in the chameleon family?

Be a lert, the command,
be a ware. I don't know what's a lert
and now they want me to be a ware.

How does one become a lert, I wonder.
Where do lerts live?
Why does everyone talk about them
as though they were real
when no one's ever seen one –
so far as I know.
And, I ask you, when
can one be a human again?
Who wants to be a lert, yellow, orange
or whatever hue?
Why do I have to be what I'm not?

I really, really, don't want to be a ware.

February 7, 2003

America the Beautiful XXVIII

When she turned 21 she shrieked and hooted
as make-up masked women strutted their bump and grind,
a male stripper took it off beneath the throbbing light,
erotica in the burlesque mode

When she turned 21 she smirked and pointed
at hooded men's uncovered erections. Some
were posed hands on heads. Prison
porn of an ugly kind.

When she turned 21 she screamed and stared
frozen at the place her legs used to be
as explosions ripped the world apart.
Naked in the most final sense
she was undone.

May 13-19, 2004

America the Beautiful XXIX

#1
insipidity
ain't
serendipity

#2
don't fuck w/my conceptions
sd the maiden to the big white bird
immaculately or other wise...
and clean up your own damn turds!

#3
mushrooms singing in the grass
send a signal as I pass
sit and sing w/us a spell
then go your way and all be well

#4
when a tree falls in a forest
and there's no one to hear the sound
being wise, the owls have to do
all the thinking so
they think so hard they fall off
their perch and are eaten by ants who
as you already know
all look like little black riding hoods.

#5
whenever I visualize affluence, I get flatulence.

April 2003/October 2005

America the Beautiful XXX

For Gene and Lauralee

Long sun shining on the west fork of the Dolores,
which means sorrow although it was a beautiful place.
Do you remember? Midsummer evening
where your dad hooked his fill, casting a line
out on the wide, swift rush, light slanting long across the flow,
approaching darkness leaning from the high peaks on either side,
deepening to dark the rushing cold where vibrant trout
jumped joyful for the last glittering bits
of light? He grilled his catch
dipped in cornmeal and oil
as around us grew silent the soft whispering chill of night.
Happy next to the kerosene stove
in the pool of hissing kerosene lamplight,
we warmed ourselves and ate the succulent dead.
Beyond the peaks, so far, the stars burned flat and helpless,
temporarily strung out on nothing,
so very bright.

Fort Bragg Winter 2004

America the Beautiful XXXI

with Sulieman Russell

Holiday Query: would you like the breast or the leg?
Staying in shape:
Stand, arms bent and kept close to the body. Pump upwards
keeping elbows behind
for at least ten repetitions of this chant (one pump for each
line, making 40 in all).
We must
We must
Improve
Our bust
Freudian Slip: "She's a breast of fresh air."
It left me breastless
Favorite C&W: "So Round, So Firm, So Fully Packed"
When all is said and done, you'll still have your mammaries
Maybe that should be nippled in the bud
Large-breasted political figure: our titular leader
Is this a case of tit for tat?
Ad: Eat At Hooters For a Titillating Experience!
An elderly stripper: Boob Saggit
Favorite salsa: Booba-lou
Have you researched the origin of the term "booboos?"
Chick flicks are known by their tittles
Riddle: What do geese, women and vehicles have in common?
(Hint: Seven letters, starts with 'H')

Let us end this little visit to the fabulous land of the boobies
with a rousing call to the
women of the world:
Boobs Up Girls, Salute the Goddess
(and remember, keep abreast of the times.)

Fort Bragg Spring 2006

America the Beautiful XXXII

Black Friday

Seven wild turkeys
Backs to the cars shushing by
Moon the revelers

2003

America the Beautiful XXXIII

for Louis Armstrong, d. April 6, 1971

by the time he left
everything we came to do was done
planted firmly on the air
a fresh breath everywhere
no him no us.
his notes spreading far and wide
ride new winds blew
all over the world and out
beyond   the stars
after that it doesn't matter what is
or what isn't done.
throw wide the windows
all the doors.
let the fresh
creation
come in.

Fort Bragg 2005

America the Beautiful XXXIV

macular degeneration
pissing on the NDN nation
whatever happened to live
and take whatever comes
and give back all of it
whatever became of mesas
soldiering on into the blue beyond

whatever happened to make
hurt, death, pain, fear
all we care about when surrounded
is beauty peace and harmony
flower sea coast village picturesque
little traffic quiet birds sly and whole
fish going about millennia
along with their sister rocks sand
salty surf, heavy seas,
keep your eyes covered
when you go out

keep your heart covered
when you walkabout
keep your tongue and your hands
to yourself
keep your head
hold your water
when does it end
where will it begin
I could do without my sight
as long as there was nothing to see
I could do without my life
as long as there was nothing to be

I could do without my heart
as long as I live or die as me
I want the NDN nation
to have another revelation
dance the old dances
sing the elder sings

Fort Bragg 2004-2007

America the Beautiful XXXV

There is another way to do something
if you think about it enough you might
figure it out

but if you think about anything
long enough nothing will get done
well or not

it's a tough call. Whether it is dark
and therefore hated
is moot because it might be bright;

bloodstained histories too far gone
make as much sense
as trying to untangle

imaginary knots in silken threads
that were never tangled –
that never were.

Some say, no thought without words;
some say, nothing at all;
some stagger across the blue, blue sky
uncertain about which way to fly – or flow

Fort Bragg October 28, 2002

America the Beautiful XXXVI

I have yet to be called soliloquy
identified as that quiet voice in the night
that whispers on the edge of hearing
a threshold of immanent possibility

going unrecognized about my daily task
serves me as well and better than any
acknowledgment however tentative
although I would name myself if you ask

and enter your awareness an obsidian blade
something else occurs each and every midnight
whether it's three a.m. or nine where you lie
I will invade your most private space

insinuate complicity in what you dare not entertain
murdering your spouse
vomiting until all poison is gone
loving unabashedly yourself walking in the rain

perhaps you think of sinister whisperings
soft wind thoughtless riffing your hair
mindful of whatever threatens
next door to death visiting

still as breath never drawn
present as emptiness and a full plate
I have been called out
named for myself confronted   undone

May 14, June 4, 2005

America the Beautiful XXXVII

tree rising over moonrise
serenades whiskey over ice.
chilling cascade of who knows when.

lost years dry as arroyos during drought,
slick as worn linoleum floors,
wishes blue as seas and skies have never been.
beyond my pane, distant howl of circling gusts wails
demise.

lately evenings seem to write epitaphs over day
reduce the years to shattered bits of porcelain broken and
bright.
trees hum their wry mysteries, twist to cacophony,
to settings that senseless, rise.

on teevee I saw the fabled white horse running free
on streets graced by dust and shimmering; I saw
that what is heat is love, is war,
is that wild to be free, white horse cantering.

I am fern, and wind canters bending me.
not so much – just limbs careless flung,
or blood-drenched dust that somehow renders life
more faceless than death. The silence and the stilled wind.
the voiceless harbingers of heat.

I who watch war flicker across my midnight screen
will never become the lightning stricken trees
that frame my life, never fling limbs so carelessly,
never run the wild streets, free.

Fort Bragg 2003

America the Beautiful XXXVIII

Two Reporters on the Scene

small pockets of resistance
hide in unexpected places.

the feyddeyin sent down
to stiffen the spines of locals

behind the blasts the call to prayer

I try to imagine the resistance as a pocket
large or small the vision eludes me.

there are always prisoners of war –
how you treat them distinguishes one from another.

the camera doesn't lie. it makes real
whatever it sees. plane and angle, light and shadow.
showing dead bodies should be proscribed
you remember there are parents out there
there are children, there are screams of grief in the night

and behind the moans the call to prayer.

images of the dead we do not show
decency demands we hide the face

so lovers and mothers won't know

towers fail and communications break up,
we see more clear the images from space

from whence the call to prayer does not arise

I didn't know until it was all said and done
keep in mind that everybody dies
behind the images, the call to prayer.

Fort Bragg 2004

There is
Another
Shore

The Kingdom of Nye

it's too late to write poems
too late to do anything but listen
to Art Bell broadcasting from the Kingdom of Nye,
suddenly returned from the Philippines
where he's moved in exhaustion and grief. lonely,
I never thought to near "This is Art Bell
from the High Desert" again, my delight, his
surprise. I vacillate between being interested
and getting furious. depends on what he has to say,
what his guests are on about.
tonight it's predictions for 2007:
one guy reports that
whales will be singing new messages, ones
we might understand, oh, how people want to know.

I'm all why can't they hear the land, the flowers,
the grass, the trees? why
not the clouds, the surf, the rocks, the stars?
you gotta wonder about people who can't hear mountains' songs,
didn't know the meadows talk to themselves and each other.
such are those who angst about a dying planet,
wail their gory *terrorismes* haven't they heard?
the sky fell a long time ago. its
rotted corpse is all they've left
don't they know they grieve their own lost souls?
Art doesn't know that we're relieved he's returned
not because we didn't like his broadcasts from
the other side of Grandmother Ocean but
because it's the High Desert speaks to us through him.
sad he doesn't know the Kingdom of Nye brought him home.
(and yet, I know he knows)

myself, I've been exiled too awhile,
grief and exhaustion bringing me low
to live at the corner of McFearless and Fear.
the fire that wiped out my life
and a lot of of my ancestral records as well,
took my entire library – all those lies. yet
today I discovered the inner voice I've been hearing
was new: another Master Teacher, formidable, this
female, imperious one. YIKES. I guess
she replaced one who taught me about Phoenix rising,
the heat, the sick nausea that ensues, as he left.
the ancient book in which I found his name
was lost too in the flames.

I love the desert, high and low, wish I lived there sometimes
like now in winter, when it blooms. but
glad enough to be still near the beach,
hearing Grandmother Ocean
mutter to herself a few blocks west of me,
where I sit and listen to Art and New Year almost here at last,
the All American Party going on in the City of Sin
not too far from the Kingdom of Nye.
let's hear it for bells and firecrackers
which I haven't heard
the frontyard cats are lonely.
I think their humans left them bereft.
after all it's New Year's Eve.

Fort Bragg, New Year's Eve 2006

Three

What We Talked About At Home

It was always rain
Did it, didn't it and where
Pouring in buckets
Falling steady sinking deep
Bare feet stepping soft drum beats

Visitor at Dusk

Strange in the twilight
Bear, large dog, I say, 'come here' --
A huge cat maybe
Moving closer in the grass
Grizzled visage burning bright

Traume

Dreams of hair, they say,
Mirror the state of your thought
Dark thick tangled gray
Twisting every which way
Every comb I use breaks

Fort Bragg 2002

Another Shore

there is another shore
not bordered by the sea we
know where no fish or beasts
we might name
flit beneath and stalk
the waves
there is another shore

there is another shore
one blessed by wordlessness
unfound by Adam
untenanted by any Lord
there is another shore

there is another shore
of which we cannot speak
though every human knows its place
that rocky promontory
without a name
there is another shore

once there was a song
faint to be sure but audible
to ears righteously attuned
strung out on voids
and gleaming falls
once there was a song

once there was a song
other than the one our parents
and their parents taught
a gleaming thread of melody
you can almost hear

out beyond the breaking surf
the restless arcing waves
sound clearly on another shore
over there, all but gone.

Fort Bragg 2003

Sin Verguenza (Shameless One)

I

what can fill the space
the hole that stays empty
no matter what's thrown into it
you can cover it for a time,
a minute or a few –
but before you know
there it is, empty, vast, silent.
how do you confront emptiness –
silence that is so total you know
it will never respond no matter
what you say. you can weep, moan,
shriek or stay quiet as can be,
it remains unmoved.
there is a certain horror about it all,
as unmet and unspecified as the person
behind the name
an empty gap that writhes with unknowns –
with danger beyond despair
when you glance or stare,
you see nothing at all, not even the void...
you hear nothing, not even the silence.
there are no words to capture this state,
no treaties, no pacts, that will make it docile
recognizable, named.
it never goes away it hovers
just out of sight ... never out of mind,
and you can't leave your mind to escape,
leave it far behind. no wish will transfer
it from here to never was; no planes fly
away from the horror space.
nobody knows its name

I know that emptiness, but only
from the edge of sight
I think I have heard its song,
but only in a never-created ear.
I recognize the despair, the fear, that
they are mine. I recognize
it will never go away. even though they did.

II

one thing I know
blowing smoke up your como se llama
is a comfort you can't deny –
or you can, and be damned yourself.
whatever leaves, whatever comes,
all of it goes up in smoke
it says so in the bible or somewhere
similar: ashes to ashes, dust to dust
as Fr. Piety prayed over us,
anointing our brows
with the gritty ashes of our sinful state.

the recognition of futility is all that is required;
when you try and try and she says,
"can't is a word that never does"
you hear 'you're no good, you
ninny, you panty-waist'. she didn't say
'effete intellectual pinko pervert who
lifts pinky holding fragile tea cup,'
but she might as well,
I got the drift long before I knew
queer and secret, taunt and shame.

there she sat pointing to the hole in my underpants
which I wore independent of other clothing.

must have been summer and warm.
Hush' tche Johnny, clan uncle, was there
she pointed at my rear, said
"the rising sun" and they laughed
complicit; it must have been 1944.
I was sniffling, as I force-scrubbed
the calcimined wall of my Crayola musings
which, like trimming the cat's whiskers,
was something you didn't do,
so I couldn't run away but instead
endured, learning that stoic way
for which my people are renowned.

shame is the counter of each and every day.

May 10-15, 2005

Wayward Girl's Lament

for Cara

The trouble when you think outside the box
is, from above you see how close the sides
and realize how bogus are the locks

you had believed could keep you safe from hawks
the name for fear they taught you cradleside;
they're troubled when you think outside the box.

Fear grows, you find you can't go back to talk,
you beckon those still huddling down inside
to realize how bogus are the locks.

They find their lives are good, intently orthodox --
sad wolves and bears who've been too long inside:
their trouble? They won't think outside the box.

Soon, while you laugh and dance beyond, they plot
to lure you in and force your compromise:
you must forget how bogus are the locks.

Wise, you won't come near their shadow box
though you're aware refusal is suicide.
It's trouble when you think outside the box
and realize how bogus are the locks

February 15, 2005

Skyscape

Did you ever want to see flying
a condor, an eagle, an albatross?

questioned the logic of our situation,
what we make of it? to seem to be,

understanding that all you know
imagines you as something else?

the dream the other night when I saw
flying in crowds around me,

heads tucked into chests tilted
to the side so I could see –

oh, look at that huge eagle
which turned out to be a pelican

feathers thick and white
bright beak gold, each winking at me

what does science make of this –
dream birds that fly, wings closed?

Fort Bragg

values

(with thanks to Henry Reed)

right now we have the value thing. in the past
we had vision. later maybe
we will have shame, guilt, rage, grief. but right now,
right now we have the values thing. hummingburds
dart about like jewels on invisible wings
and right now we have the value thing.

this is the word of Jesus. and this
is the law of Jehovah, whose work you will know
in his wrathful fires and this is the resolve
of the C.E.O. in D.C. which in our case we didn't choose.
the deer wander quiet over the rise, grazing on whatever's there,

this is the situation: grave in the extreme.
redemption can only be gained by pulverizing waves
of stealthy bombing. please do not try to find haven
in laughing, dancing, waving angry signs. you must
realize that selective massacre is our god-fearing choice. the
daffodils that cluster in the tiny sanctuary just beyond the fence
give no thought to their salvation.

and this you can see is the reason: god is good
and evil is what we despise. the value
of a just war is manifest: to free the enslaved, to heal
their pain and to load them on the value train of salvation.
a huge, fat bee probes a shadowed cluster of purple blooms
repeatedly piercing tender light spilling centers with surgical strikes.
this is called liberating pollen for the hive

we call it liberating pollen for our lives; it's hard
to think about, harder for us to do, but god has commanded:

there but for me goes the least of you. the path has been made clear
by Jehovah, Jesus, Paul, born again President who thinks he's a king,
hierophants who lead us in righteousness, which in our case
we didn't choose. at dusk the birds make their steady way home
to nestle and mumble into sleep as the silenced world flows into dark,
and today we have the value thing.

Still Crazy

It was then as it is now
just as the holy men say
although they took that page
from the Book of Old Wives Tales.

Whatever. I say it works
the same now as it did then
even with all the proud
information that dangles – free radical
deconstructing our realities
that made the world seem solid
since before our time.

Then, was I in that thirty-second year
when one knows little enough...
except I wanted the ugly, the unpleasant,
the vicious to just go away. I thought
wishing and willing would make it so.

I got pregnant that summer, nineteen seventy-one

Ecstatic in the full-bodied sight and sound
of the great thunder kachina
like gods they were
towering golden in the sky
high above Gallup
New Mexico.

But the winter I was thirty two
I was smack up against truth:
crippling effects of pregnancy,

six weeks in bed, birth
of blessed twins full of light
one dead two exact months after his birth.

There I was, feeling secure,
believing that one god, one man, one world
would make of everything good enough for me –
even the pain

I had no idea what pain could be.

Fort Bragg 2002

Self Portrait and a Wish

I don't much go for action,
the speedy joke, quick, sharp wit –
don't go straight toward the goal.
I am an old Laguna Pueblo Indian – poet
ADDle-brain, raised good Catholic girl. I
hover around the edges, discern
shadowed shapes in between. I
like my lighting indirect –
think sun is brutal, seek
the blessed shade. Being so,
I lie in wait, a sedentary bitch.
I have ditch water in my veins just
like the US Senator over a hundred years ago
accused Pueblos and the Spaniards who had lived
among them four hundred years – but how
I wish I was action-packed, loaded for bear,
right on kind of girl.

March 2004

Dawn Sneaks

The dawn sneaks up puffing broad with hubris
trying to make me believe it has something to do with me
something that will lift me to a realm beyond fantasy.
But all I have to do is squint, close my eyes a second,
to realize that softness is a covert glare, not splendor but rage,
there is no hope of humility, no companion there.

Dawn is no fool and neither am I. Hubris is a trait
I may well share – it's certain I have my fantasy
of singularity above everything that creeps below, a second
here or there, maybe a whole lot more, and rage:
that I'll own. Still I have learned when it's me sidling slow
as though no one there could be aware that charm is rage,

intent upon my aggrandizement, hubris
drives me, not humility. My way
or rot, that grand fantasy composed equally
of rage and immaturity that can obliterate nations
without a second chance, any idea of difference –
make living richer, deeper; place something there.

Between the me and thee, the this and some other thing
as open as sky and sea in the second where they meet –
which, one can say, has its own hubris
to be sure – taken there as a whole rather than a multitude
of compositions ever almost meeting, halted in the grasp of rage,
infinity of never-entering, a space-time warp of fantasy.

Unrealizing openness as surely causes crafty silent rage
as closing mind to sense of other days. The sign of hubris,
its inevitability of tragic endings in real time as well as fantasy,
enamored exactly of itself, there struts upon a mindless stage

in idiotic self-examining narration, not a second thought for one
       another,
insinuates sure suggestion: it's only me, hypnotic, lovely, love me
       only me –

No. It seems to me dawn's as much of fantasy as blazing noon
and then some. Hubris has its wiles, its beauty-spendored rage.
Yet there is something other there – that moment: almost born,
       forever free.

Fort Bragg 2004

I Understand When I Watch TV

The commercial asks if my dreams are calling me,
giving me pause to realize indeed they are,
they do, flitting about the corners of awareness,
softly, barely registered, "Paula, Paula!"
enticing images pass too quick snatched away.

Puts me in mind of my mother's voice echoing
across the Cubero hills, sandstone mesas Teresa and I
wandered in the days when freedom meant
"Go outside and play." We climbed the Chinese elm trees in my yard,
lay on the grass and dreamed, made visions out of great clouds passing
overhead, busy about their lives, sometimes heard them muttering
almost too soft to hear.

My future is mostly in the past, and the present
flickers by quick as cat paws for bird, too quick for mind or eye.
I arise, the day goes wherever days go and it's night.
By bits and bobs my life drifts away, poom, poom,
and Bob's your uncle, as the cousins say.
And what happened to the years?

I remember all the tears, all the sturm und drang, can
barely fathom what all the fuss was about
then as now. I know more who walk on the dead side,
more "passed on" as grandma and mother would say
than I know this side of the grave –
Makes a woman lonely, and there's little can assuage
really, although I laugh a lot and fall in love
each moment at the birds flittering outside my sliding door
the flowers bobbing their delighted heads,
the trees deep song, the huge
grandmother and grandfather rocks on the beach and along the roads,
ponderous moaning timeless songs.

Coyote rhymester on the lam

jacking all tradesters
mastering none
disillusion fading
enter the sun

never portraying
forever sunk
morning comes flailing
some, all and none

all's cool the ends
cruel or stubborn or bereft
headfuck words suck
shit rhymes end of time
bobby shaftoe's gang aglee
auld bobby burns lang syne free

to be forgiven shrunk and shriven
centuries mock the ticktock clock
and all the has-beens blow to sea
each asking each who they used to be

lyre liar britches on fire
dying cat tied to a can
fire brigade edging up a tree
howling feline who won't be freed

never mind nobody's there
to even wonder nor ever care
I wish I was a wave at sea
a sandy beach a poplar tree

a way to straggle, fine way to be
no better than you if you could see
if you'd remember you've never been
and never would want to truth could be

better be buying better be sold
no use in trying for swift or bold
stupid legends we give all to sing
never once grokking to ravens caws
claws snatching shreds flesh quaking

it's not a matter of what it means
a poem shouldn't mean but be
life is meaningless thank the lord
I think and so i'll never be

just as well any poet would know
when cradle's rocking the storms
blow and blow, candles dance and flutter
then they go out, enter the dark
that's what it's all about

birds of a feather flock together
and they begin to cry
tucking their wee heads
into their wings forgetting they ever
knew how to fly
they think they remember
what it is to dream
poor poor birdies,
poor poor things

Fort Bragg 2002

All the Same Beans

beans, beans, human beans
yellow and white and red and pink
three bean salad, beans in a pot,
beans beans, all the same beans

growing and glowing
blowing seeds around
dropping and drooping
blooming and dying
beans, beans, all the same beans

human beans fighting
human beans loving
human beans writing
human beans grieving
beans, beans all the same beans

take some beans
put em in a pot
spotted beans, black beans,
garbanzo beans, the lot
beans, beans all the same beans

soak them simmer them
add a bit of hog
dried beans, butter beans
perhaps a bit of squash

beans beans human beans
green and black
and pinto and white
dried, fresh, soy, navy, lime
beans, beans all the same beans

beans love the fire's heat
beans love the light
give them back their water
and they love the drying part
beans, beans, all the same beans

and when they're soft
and almost squishy done
salt them, pepper them
mash them with a spoon
beans, beans all the same beans

you might use butter
you might use ghee
you might use olive oil

onions, chili, beef
beans, beans, all the same beans

sound the gong
ring the bell
bang the drum
. supper's on
beans, beans, all the same beans

water them, fire them, eat them for three days
wham! bam! magic, man!
beans to gas, gas to light
light to fire, fire to stars —
beans, beans all the same beans

Fort Bragg, August 2002

Which Way's Up, Doc?

Unlike Bugs Bunny,
Having turned left at Albuquerque
like the commercial advises us to do,
we came to see
purple hills reflecting purple waves
azure surf, white white foam
off the shore of Galacia

of course no one knew
whether we had come from west
or east, so turning left
leaves a lot shall we say
unresolved.

Having turned left at the heart
of the Southwest and bypassed
the promised Seven Cities of Gold
that Santiago del Conquistador in Spain
and the knights of El Dorado wandered over land and sea
seeking, always seeking we come at last to these,
purpled horizon on azure surf, golden sand on empty beach,
wondering about those who legend say came ashore just here
we gaze amazed at the purple branches of low lying shrubs
a few hundred yards distant on the rise above our heads
just where the beach becomes a Spanish town, the name of
      which I forget
but I am struck all these years since by the light
the significance to tales far from cathedrals and pilgrims' roads
I can't help but wonder:
there is so much gold in these sands, these skies,
what made soldiers, priests and gold-seekers
come across the terrible seas, then march for fifty years north
      to my home,

right before Albuquerque was anything other
than a Duke, content enough in his stony battlements in this
ancient place.

Borrachitarme Voy

It isn't as though anyone
listened much in those days –
in movies slinky post-War women wore
tight-woven soft black straw hats
lightly brimmed, alluring veiled,
and post-War girls wore shiny black patent leather shoes.
Inside their soles Buster boys and magic frogs
plucked promises that only Let's Pretend could keep.
Halcyon days of Ralston and Cream of Wheat
were not at all like these where everything up
for grabs goes tediously unresolved. Still
alfalfa fields nod quiet in the blaze of July sun,
and arroyos flood sudden violence down down
and never reach the wine-drunk sea.
Every season someone's brother drowns.

SE FUE [He Left (Himself)]

For Gene

A month. And some days.
Losses mount in my drying yard.
Along with the grass, mare's tails,
coastal plants whose names I don't know,
there are the birds.
If I keep feeding them they come.

Somewhere others will be laughing –
dancing, getting drunk, *musicos* serenading them
among the graves. Somewhere
la gente will mount marigolds, before the photos of their dead,
light candles, set out photographs of *los muertos,*
strategically place bottles of booze,
plates of *pans dulces,* other blooms on the *offrenda.*
The marigolds will fall in a tumble all the way
to the open door. *Bien venidos.* Welcome.

You used to tell outlandish tales
or play your songs murmuring
over the strings until you had me
in tears. I don't know how
to dance with the dead, or offer
tequila, marigolds, *dulces,* sweets.
But I can say, *mihito,* my son.
Come home.

Fort Bragg 2003

Minding the Gap

over Noyo Harbor they're building something
maybe it's an extension of the bridge.
I heard a rumor to that effect before
I moved up here. bridge is good;
it's harder to get from here to there
without one.
the bridge they're working on
spans the gulf
between there an here;
seagulls and seals like being there,
turkey vultures hang close by.
lovers and other seekers
stop on the cliffs it spans
just around the cliff"s curve along the waterside
I used to be a bridge from here to elsewhere –
had no idea that bridge-being entailed
lifting here, reaching there,
prop it on your hip up and over you go,
hang over thin air and never tire;
the ones who crossed me were mostly
oblivious. I didn't mind
I minded a lot
few notice a bridge, where it begins,
where it ends, how much faith it implies.
intent on destinations,
what stretches between is a means whereby.
seabirds circle, land, sit on the rails
meditate on fish
humans pass them by.
weighing tons, we swish our way over thin air
a hundred feet above water,
hunched over steering, radios on blare.
just now changes coerce attention; we decry

inconvenience, delay, unsightly cranes.
sometimes amazed and always a bit scared
I drive nearly a half ton of me across the the gap,
sometimes quick, sometimes slow it's a matter
of faith I say – in engineering, in construction,
in at least one dead man's body
entombed in the piling –
that they work together to hold up the sky.

March 2, 2004

Treasured

the night the velvet the black sky
the deeper than obsidian the silken veil
ebony rain drifting
through the void entering vastness
spate of drops gust beyond cold
 I cannot touch anything other than air
finer than midnight so it is
far off crosses the dark mesas
bisects stately the fragrant plain
disappears over the ridge of night
deep as mourning
tight and flicked with spattered light
transitory pure nothing
as clean as star lost rain
absent sky

Fort Bragg, October 5, 2007

Love Poem

for Khu Saht

it must have been august on a shiny day
the kind that fools you into thinking all's okay
except if you're noticing there's ice behind the wind.

it might have been some starry night, individualities blurred
by star dust – the kind Frank Sinatra et al used to threnodize --
or even a harvest moon drifting over a cloudy sky.

whatever it was it occasioned love poems and hands clasped
tight and childhood lips pressed together amidst fiery starfall
as if remembering our original creation from a parental asteroid,
80% clay, 20% water crashed before the oceans were born,

those oceans we sail and surf and sing about now. whenever,
it was too long ago to remember properly, to construct
primal time when love came into a heart I might claim as mine
supposing I knew there was an I, an eye, an islet in the salt salt sea.

it must have been dawn when the face of beauty first entered me
and made the first child of god, child of glad, daughter of sunrise,
of yellow corn, of soft wind – still chill but with warmth behind;
or after midnight when the velvet dark was starry-eyed -
who knows? who could even care over eons so vast the mind staggers
derelict down the slummiest, most sacred streets of forever.

it might have been fantasy born of longing, loss, regret, anguish --
the kind that time and fate bring to everyone – cats, trees, worms,
you, me – as if a longing so sharp could last 4.5 billion years or so,
as though memory ever clear could outlast glaciation, global warming,
a million years' rain, and millions of years of thrusting fire.

who are you I love, I need with all my being, the one I cannot
forget, lose sight of – for all my whining, sighing, joking around?
what is that flickering astonishment of tiny blue lights stabbing out of
a deep black veil that beaks my heart?
some call it god, but I know it's not,
he's not you, you're not him...not so great a mystery as that,
but so far, still.

Fort Bragg, January 2008

How Near, How Far

A fine spring day in the East Bay.
The first this year. I am preoccupied
realizing exactly that what slouched
toward the White Sands
to be born is grown, already
getting old. I'm driven to get out
while the sun shines
in a calmer city a life away from Trinity,
a place smugly self-satisfied place
from whence it came, a place
where the perfect sun gets tangled
in the branches of predictably ho-hum trees,
where whatever it is that I've
been dreaming lies asleep,
making everything
I recognize a bit too late –
that that's okay. I did find out
what's in a name, by god,
and I gotta say it isn't much.
Still, a good ol' rummage of 50's junk
piled high in a second-hand store's
a trip, listening to adolescent songs, Toni Grant,
Chubby Checkers, Little Richard, Les Paul
and Mary Ford. Look, some Navajo rugs,
prices pretty good; look formica and chrome tables,
monstrosities of my ill-spent youth
as young married in Grants, New Mexico
a generation and a half ago; look,
aluminum glasses that made your reeth ache
when you used them to drink ice tea. It's
a rush, this spring walk through self-recovery land,
though I discover few if any
homey bargains in the heaps.

I'm reminded that whatever glitters
isn't gold, and nothing ever smells as sweet,
however faint the music,
however high the moon.

Berkeley, CA 1999

A Note on the Text

It may be that the hardest book to edit is that of a friend who's already passed on. Paula's long connection with my wife Pat Smith and her briefer one (only twenty years!) with me left both of us, as deepest friendships often do, unprepared for her departure. Several times during her last few years she sent us batches of poems, for readings at which she would be absent or as markers along the way; she mailed the full manuscript of *America the Beautiful* to us on May 20, 2008, nine days before her death. The note inside said simply, "The picture of the eagle is for the cover of my book. The book was sent to me, for you."

Our two-year pause in publishing this book can be attributed to several causes: early grief, the pressure of prior commitments to publish, and lingering questions we had about some of the poems themselves. We kept wanting to go back to Paula and ask her what she thought. Finally we realized we'd have to answer those as best we could.

The result could never be perfect. Paula herself might have further revised some poems. In the first section, the series "America the Beautiful," inevitably some poems seemed less developed than others. We omitted a very few of these and renumbered the sequence. Scholars interested in the missing poems may contact us. In the second section, which we titled "There Is Another Shore" from the first line of a poem, we included a few pieces that might not have survived a more orderly volume. We wanted to preserve Paula's moods and impulses, with some poems personal and close to home, some chiding, mournful, or strident about an America that never had fulfilled its promise, some close to word games with a touch of the frivolous. Paula's work could be complicated and contradictory: we left that in.

Our thanks to her daughter Lauralee Brown and Paula's other family members and friends, including those who honored her life at the Diego Rivera Center at San Francisco City College on October 25, 2008. On this end, our thanks to Gloria Williams, who copied the manuscript and assisted us in the editing; to Bryce Milligan, ever the spirit behind the layout and design; and my own thanks to Pat Smith, Paula's devoted editor and friend, without whom I might have missed the wonderful experience of knowing Paula altogether.

John Crawford, Publisher
West End Press
May, 2010

Postscript: To our great sorrow, my wife Patricia Clark Smith died July 11 of this year of organ failure. She was 67. Pat's best memorial is her love of other people, expressed in so many ways, as it is in her preface to this volume. I miss her terribly and many others do as well. A forthcoming edition from West End Press will consist of Pat's uncollected writings; her note on Paula is the last finished piece she wrote.

August, 2010